INSIDE THE MORGAN

Pierpont Morgan's Study

Jennifer Tonkovich

The Morgan Library & Museum, New York

Library of Congress Cataloging-in-Publication
Data: A catalogue record for this book is available
from the publisher.
ISBN: 978-0-87598-178-9

Printed in the United States of America

Front cover: Pierpont Morgan's study, 2016
Back cover: Pierpont Morgan's study, 1925

Published by the Morgan Library & Museum
Karen Banks, *Publications Manager*
Patricia Emerson, *Senior Editor*
Eliza Heitzman, *Editorial Assistant*

Project Staff
Jennifer Tonkovich, *Eugene and Clare Thaw Curator,*
Department of Drawings and Prints
Giada Damen, *Moore Curatorial Fellow,*
Department of Drawings and Prints
Marilyn Palmeri, *Imaging and Rights Manager*
Graham S. Haber, *Photographer*

Designed by Jo Ellen Ackerman /
Bessas & Ackerman
Typeset in Monotype Baskerville
Printed on McCoy Silk Text and bound by
Puritan Capital

Contents

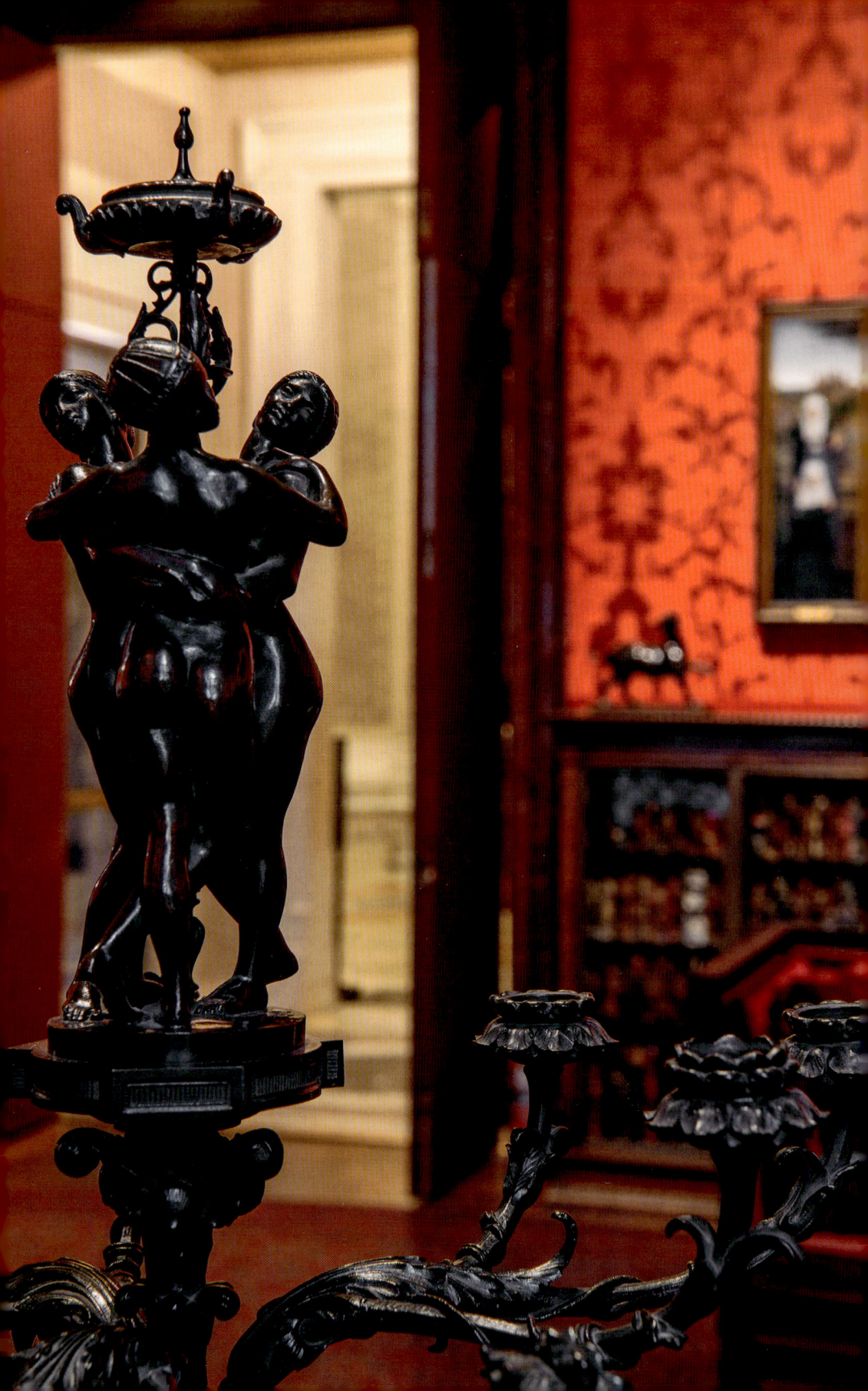

Director's Foreword

In 1902, with his collection of rare books and manuscripts overflowing the basement of his brownstone at the corner of Madison Avenue and 36th Street, John Pierpont Morgan (1837–1913) telephoned the architect Charles Follen McKim of the firm McKim, Mead, and White to commission a freestanding library adjacent to his home. McKim created a building that is a hallmark of the American Renaissance style and in 1966 was designated a National Historic Landmark.

Once the building was completed in 1906, Morgan spent much of his remaining years in this richly appointed private study, away from the Wall Street offices of his banking firm. Here, among some of his favorite works of art, Morgan worked, relaxed, and met with art dealers and business associates. It was in this room that he gathered a group of bankers in November 1907 to orchestrate a dramatic resolution to a national financial panic. In keeping with the neo-Renaissance style of his new library, Morgan adorned his study with a selection of carefully chosen paintings and sculptures by Italian and Northern Renaissance masters as well as treasured volumes of English literature.

Today, Morgan's presence is embodied by a portrait mounted above the fireplace, depicting the fifty-two-year-old banker in 1888, as he was about to embark on his career as one of the world's leading art collectors. Nearby, between the windows, hangs a portrait of his son, J. P. Morgan, Jr. (1867–1943), painted in 1934, a decade after the founding of the Morgan Library. The younger Morgan was responsible for making the exceptional collections assembled by his father, which he continued to augment, accessible to the public.

Colin B. Bailey, *Director*

Inside Morgan's Study   JENNIFER TONKOVICH

Once the banker John Pierpont Morgan (1837–1913) and his architect, Charles Follen McKim (1847–1909), settled on a Renaissance-style villa for his new library adjacent to his brownstone on 36th Street, construction of the exterior began in earnest in April 1903. In addition to a dazzling marble entrance hall, a two-story library housing thousands of volumes, and an office for Morgan's librarian, McKim's plans for the library included a private study intended as the banker's reception room and personal retreat. Morgan's biographer and son-in-law, Herbert Satterlee, said that no one could really know Morgan if they had not seen him "seated in silence before the fire in his study, smoking a large black cigar, perusing the latest acquisition or playing solitaire." From the beginning of the project, Morgan played a vital role in determining the appearance of the room and in selecting objects to adorn it, a process that lasted the remainder of his life.

In early 1904, as construction of the building progressed and the walls were reaching the cornice, McKim turned his attention increasingly to the interior. The process of designing the four principal interiors began in February 1904 and would continue even after completion of the building at the start of 1906. McKim's initial proposal for Morgan's study (now the West Room) was dramatically different from what we see today: an early watercolor reveals the interior hung with wall coverings depicting verdant gardens populated with exotic birds (Fig. 1). A cornice with moldings in white and gold on a blue background runs above the tapestries; this stucco decoration links the study with the entrance hall and library, both of which have ceilings featuring sculpted decorations. A hint of the room's eventual crimson hue is found in the deeply colored and dramatically veined marble that surrounds the windows. McKim's initial scheme was eventually abandoned in favor of red

FIG. 1

fabric-covered walls above the bookshelves, an idea inspired by the wall coverings in Joseph Widener's art gallery at Lynnewood Hall.

The West Room's silk-covered walls are one of the most striking elements of Morgan's study; they establish the luxurious atmosphere and vibrant palette (Fig. 2). The damask design incorporates the insignia of the Chigi, a Renaissance banking family originally from Siena, and comprises a cluster of six *monti*, or mountains, and an eight-pointed star. Perhaps the most celebrated member of the family was Agostino Chigi (1466–1520), a banker and patron of the arts who was the richest man in Rome during his lifetime. It is not surprising to find that the Chigi emblem was chosen since Agostino's villa, now known as the Farnesina, was an important inspiration for the decorative program of the library ceiling.

As in the entrance hall and library, the ceiling was critical to the decoration of the room. Plans for it underwent several changes during the development phase that occupied much of 1904. An early elevation shows a domed ceiling with a central skylight. In May, McKim noted that Morgan preferred a flat ceiling to a vaulted one for his study. It was soon decided that the room needed an antique ceiling, and McKim began searching for one in earnest. At last, in March 1905, the Florentine dealer Stefano Bardini (1836–1922) sent a sample that contained some elements of a carved ceiling likely dating to the sixteenth century; those elements served as the basis for a ceiling that a team of craftsmen would construct that summer.

FIG. 2

FIG. 3

Unfortunately, Morgan was not apprised of the ceiling's creation before a tour of the building with the painter Harry S. Mowbray (1858–1928) in September 1905. Morgan was unhappy to find that the West Room deviated from the plans he had seen and that McKim had made changes without his approval. During their inspection, according to Mowbray, "the storm burst over Morgan's own private room—in which there was no color as yet—and moreover the ceiling (a Bardini antique) was totally different from the one that figured in the plans. We did the rest of the inspection under a thundercloud." (Fortunately Morgan's mood improved when he entered the library.) After the ceiling had been installed, it needed to be lowered one foot so that it would better fit the proportions of the room, leaving roughly eight feet of space between the ceiling and the roof. Once the ceiling was in place, James Wall Finn (1866–1913), the artist responsible for the ceiling paintings in the librarian's office (now the North Room) nearby, was charged with enhancing the wood with painted decorations that were intended to evoke Renaissance-era ceilings. Decorative elements used by Finn include grotesque masques, zodiac symbols (a crab; several armed centaurs, perhaps representing Sagittarius), and female figures. His embellishments, along with the eventual installation of the wall fabric, introduced color and texture to the initially austere room (Fig. 3).

Another essential element of Morgan's study is the fireplace that forms the focal point of the room (Fig. 4). The library, librarian's office, and study all have mantels chosen by Morgan on a visit to Florence and agreed to by McKim in May 1904, and each incorporates earlier elements and contempo-

FIG. 4

FIG. 5

rary craftsmanship. The dark stone lintel is a work of Renaissance carving. The motif features a central shield lacking the expected heraldic emblems or coat of arms, suggesting it once awaited a buyer. The shield is encircled by a garland of palms and flanked by cupids, according to fifteenth-century fashion. Long described as the work of the Florentine master sculptor Desiderio da Settignano (ca. 1428–1464), the lintel is now attributed to his talented pupil Francesco di Simone Ferrucci (1437–1493). The brackets and two pillars are also antiques, as are the pilasters ornamented with bas-reliefs of pine, poppies, and foliage, although they do not all date from the same time. The remaining elements of the chimneypiece were constructed by Venetian craftsmen to blend the antique and modern elements together seamlessly.

To illuminate the room, McKim included two tall, vertical windows on the west wall and a window higher up on the north wall, all clad in a robust red marble, called *griotte,* which originates in the south of France, the Pyrenees, and southern Belgium (Fig. 5). The same marble was imported by the Romans and popular in France during the eighteenth century (it was used for the mantel in the office of Louis XIV at Versailles). In McKim's early watercolors, the windows throughout the building are set with clear panes, affording a view outside and abundant natural light. Eventually, the decision was made to add to the windows inset panels of vibrantly colored stained glass, which would leave no surface without ornamentation. Beginning in 1904, Morgan began collecting panes of stained glass. It was not until 1907, however, that all of the windows in the building were removed and inset with the colorful panes; the process took two years. Eventually, stained-glass fragments were incorporated into the windows in the study, office, and library as well as in incidental spaces like the vault and the back door. The scenes range in date from the fifteenth through the seventeenth centuries and include works from England, Germany, Switzerland, France, and the Low Countries. Adding to the illumination in the study is an elegant alabaster chandelier adorned with bronze sphinxes, fitted for electric lighting. It was designed by Edward F. Caldwell (1851–1914), New York's preeminent manufacturer of light fixtures and decorative metalwork during the Gilded Age. Given Morgan's well-known support of Thomas Edison and electric lighting, it is not surprising that Caldwell's elegant gilt fixtures are found throughout the library.

Security was critical to Morgan, especially with his treasures concentrated in a well-publicized, gleaming new building. By January 1907, he had a night watchman and engineer on staff, and by 1908 an electronic burglar alarm system had been installed by the Holmes Electric Protective Company.

A bank-style steel vault was even incorporated into the original design of the study (Fig. 6). McKim conceived the idea of a vault, concealed behind steel doors covered with "a false wooden door or paneling," where Morgan would store his most valuable manuscripts. The half-inch-steel-lined vault initially consisted of one tier of metal shelving, with a second tier accessed by a rolling ladder that was added in 1906. The metal platform and stairs were installed during the 1960s. The vault received natural illumination via a large window on the south end, which, as with all the building's fenestration, was equipped with a securable bronze fire shutter on the inside and an iron grill on the exterior. This stronghold was used to house the collection of manuscripts—medieval and Renaissance, and literary and historical—from Morgan's day until 2003. It now contains a selection of the luxurious volumes Morgan commissioned to document his varied collections as well as finely tooled cases that once housed manuscripts.

Morgan was also particular about the furniture for his study (Fig. 7). In London, A. Barnard Cowtan, of the firm Cowtan and Sons, agonized over getting the details right. Cowtan reminded Morgan's librarian, Belle da Costa Greene (1883–1950), that he needed time to execute the high-quality carving required for so many sizable objects. The large order placed in late 1906 nearly overwhelmed Cowtan's shop. He had well over a hundred men working "nearly all night" in December 1906 to ensure Morgan would receive a furniture shipment by the start of the new year. The robust lion's-paw feet on the desk, chairs, and settee were derived from Renaissance examples in the South Kensington Museum, such as a walnut cassone made for Cosimo I de Medici (1519–1574) in the 1560s. Morgan's desk was fitted with a leather top containing his intertwined initials embossed in gold, and featured spring-push panels and concealed drawers for storing sensitive material.

Not everything went smoothly. The size of the settee caused a minor uproar: the original piece was rejected for being too dainty. Cowtan chronicled the progress on a new one, "The big settee to take the place of the one rejected by Mr. Morgan is not quite finished yet but shall be sent out shortly, and this time we have not erred on the small side, and it should look very handsome across the fireplace in his own room." At last the piece was shipped in November 1907, when Cowtan wrote to lament, "There is no necessity to go into the details of the anxiety that I have gone through in respect of this piece of furniture." By the end of Morgan's first year in the building, his study was nearly fully furnished.

Perhaps the most distinguishing feature in Morgan's study is that the room is lined with a tier of deep bookcases, in which he installed his collection of early English printed books, amounting to nearly three thousand volumes,

FIG. 6

and including his precious tomes by William Caxton (ca. 1422–ca. 1491), who is celebrated as the first book printer and seller in England. These bookcases, and their counterparts in the library, are made of walnut delicately ornamented with golden-hued applewood inlays and protected by lockable, openwork bronze grills. The deep tops of the shelves allowed for the display of objects (or, as Morgan's nephew Junius called them, bric-a-brac) and storage of folio volumes and left the walls free for Morgan to hang paintings. One innovation is concealed in the cases to the left of the fireplace, where a series of shallow shelving units slide on a track to reveal a second layer of shelves behind. These shelves offered storage space where Morgan kept titles that were of a private nature, such as André Robert de Nerciat's *Le diable au corps* (1786),

FIG. 7

Théophile Gautier's *Mademoiselle de Maupin* (1835), and *Felicia: A Novel* (1891) by Fanny Noailles Dickinson Murfee. The contents of these shelves were sold by Morgan's son in 1915, two years after his death.

Morgan's study, with its deep shelves, richly carved tables, and damask walls, provided the proprietor with the opportunity to display his finest works of art, incorporating the advantages of a gallery into his library. These paintings and sculptures joined an abundance of furniture in the room, from Islamic mother-of-pearl inlaid chairs to Renaissance stools and tables, all arranged on a mid-nineteenth-century carpet from southeast Turkestan in hues of gray and purple (now replaced by a modern replica). The interior had a Victorian richness, and a glimpse of the original distribution of objects can be seen in the only image of the study taken during Morgan's lifetime (Fig. 8): a color photograph produced in 1912 by Arnold Genthe (1869–1942), who considered the study "the most beautiful room in America."

18

During the building's construction, Morgan retained objects from some of the larger collections that he had purchased and acquired individual objects of importance for his study. He also began a focused campaign to acquire paintings by Renaissance artists to adorn his walls, charging agents abroad to identify potential purchases. With the tone of the interior set in the entrance hall and library by the neo-Renaissance style mural paintings, which pay homage to masters such as Raphael (1483–1520) and Pinturicchio (ca. 1452–1513), Morgan specifically sought examples of early Renaissance painting in a similar clear, linear style and vibrant hues. It took several years to accumulate the pictures seen in some of the earliest images of Morgan's study, with each year from 1907 until 1913 bringing new additions to the room (and new arrangements to the walls).

Today, visitors to Morgan's study can experience this Gilded Age interior up close, reveling in the luxurious atmosphere in which Morgan spent the last years of his life, surrounded by some of the most beautiful objects he collected.

FIG. 8

WORKSHOP OF FERRER BASSA (SPANISH, ACTIVE CA. 1324–48)
Polyptych with Scenes from the Life of Christ, the Life of the Virgin, and Saints, ca. 1345–50
Tempera on panel

An excellent example of Gothic painting from Catalonia, this polyptych has been recently attributed to the workshop of Ferrer Bassa. It may have been executed by Bassa's son Arnau based on Ferrer's design. Evocative of contemporary Italian painting, the four panels of this altarpiece

depict scenes from the life of the Virgin (at the top), the Passion of Christ (in the center row), and saints (at the bottom). The lunettes above depict the instruments of the Passion, the mourning Virgin, Christ as the Man of Sorrows (one of the earliest examples in Spanish painting), and the mourning St. John.

BOHEMIAN SCHOOL

The Dormition of the Virgin and *The Adoration of the Magi*, ca. 1355–60
Tempera and gold on linen-covered panels

Crafted at the court of Holy Roman Emperor Charles IV (r. 1346–78) at Prague, these exquisite panels likely formed a diptych—commissioned perhaps by the emperor himself. In the scene of the three kings adoring the Christ child, the second magus has the features of Charles, and his red cloak bears the imperial eagle. In the panel depicting the Virgin's death, St. Peter wears the three-tiered papal tiara. These details allude to the delicate balance between sacred and terrestrial power.

PURCHASED BY J. P. MORGAN, JR., 1931

HANS MEMLING (FLEMISH, CA. 1440–1494)

Kneeling Female Donor with St. Anne, ca. 1467–70
Kneeling Male Donor with St. William of Maleval, ca. 1467–70
Oil on panel

Among Memling's finest early works in this country, these two panels once formed the inner wings of a triptych. They depict relatives, along with their patron saints, of Jan Crabbe, the fifteenth-century abbot who commissioned the altarpiece. At left, St. Anne stands behind an older, kneeling woman, who is probably Crabbe's mother, Anna. At right, St. William of Maleval appears in armor behind a young man, probably the abbot's half brother.

PURCHASED BY PIERPONT MORGAN, 1907

HANS MEMLING (FLEMISH, CA. 1440–1494)

Portrait of a Man with a Pink, ca. 1480–85

Oil on panel

This is one of the finest paintings Morgan acquired for his personal collection. The sitter may have been a member of the Italian merchant colony in the flourishing city of Bruges, where Memling was the leading painter. He was renowned for his skills as a portraitist, and his works were particularly preferred by foreign visitors to the city, who appreciated his meticulous realism. The pink, or carnation, in the young man's hand is a symbol of betrothal, and the letter he holds in the other may be a love letter or marriage contract, suggesting that the painting commemorates an engagement or wedding.

PURCHASED BY PIERPONT MORGAN, 1907

AFTER SANDRO BOTTICELLI (ITALIAN, 1444-45–1510)

Madonna of the Magnificat, ca. 1490

Oil on panel

This is one of more than a dozen versions made by contemporaries of Botticelli after an original that the artist painted ca. 1481. The many versions attest to the immediate success of Botticelli's composition and its appeal to contemporary Florentine collectors. The title derives from the opening words of the Virgin's song of exaltation, *Magnificat anima mea dominum* (My soul doth glorify the Lord), which she is writing in the book before her.

GIAN GIACOMO D'ALLADIO, CALLED MACRINO D'ALBA (ITALIAN, CA. 1465–1528)

Portrait of a Knight of Malta, 1499

Tempera on panel

The sitter wears the white cross of the Order of Malta, one of the oldest lay religious orders, whose fifteenth-century members were Catholic, of noble birth, and devoted to works of virtue and charity. He may be Benvenuto San Giorgio of Biandrate (1450–1527), a nobleman, papal ambassador, and knight of the order since 1480. The dated inscription in the border reads *By the hand of Macrino I shall live after death 1499.*

PURCHASED BY PIERPONT MORGAN, 1909

ATTRIBUTED TO MARCO BELLO (ITALIAN, CA. 1431-36–1523) AFTER GIOVANNI BELLINI (ITALIAN, CA. 1430–1516)

Virgin and Child Blessing a Kneeling Donor, with Four Saints, ca. 1500

Tempera on panel, transferred to canvas

Attributed to Marco Bello, a member of Bellini's prolific Venetian workshop, this painting was likely based on different models developed by the master. This would account for the lack of consistency in scale and placement in space of the beautifully conceived figures. The saints depicted include (left to right) Paul, George, an unidentified female saint, and an unidentified martyr, perhaps St. Cecilia, with a wreath and palm. The devotional subject and presence of a donor portrait indicate that this was a private commission.

PURCHASED BY PIERPONT MORGAN, 1910

PIETRO VANNUCCI, CALLED PERUGINO (ITALIAN, CA. 1450–1523)

Virgin and Saints Adoring the Christ Child, ca. 1500
Tempera on panel

Known for his graceful figures, Perugino, the leading Umbrian painter of his day, was Raphael's principal master. Using harmonious jewel-like tones, the artist depicted the Virgin flanked by St. John the Evangelist and an unidentified female saint, likely Mary Magdalene. The inscription on the frame, referring to the Christ child, is from Psalm 45: *Fairer in beauty are you than the sons of men; grace is poured out upon they lips; thus God has blessed you forever.*

PURCHASED BY PIERPONT MORGAN, 1911

FRANCESCO FRANCIA (ITALIAN, CA. 1450–1517)

Virgin and Child with SS. Dominic and Barbara

Oil on panel

Although trained as a goldsmith, Francia primarily worked as a painter in and around his hometown of Bologna. Depictions of the Virgin and child with saints are predominant among his major surviving works. St. Barbara is shown with a martyr's palm and a model of the tower in which her pagan father imprisoned her, while St. Dominic, the founder of the Dominican order, wears his black and white habit and holds a lily and a book. When Francia painted the present panel, he was influenced by the luminous style of his contemporary Perugino, another artist represented in Morgan's study.

PURCHASED BY PIERPONT MORGAN, 1907

GIOVANNI BATTISTA CIMA DA CONEGLIANO (ITALIAN, CA. 1460–1517-18)

Virgin and Child with SS. Catherine and John the Baptist, ca. 1515
Oil on panel

While the Christ child leans back to play with St. John the Baptist's cross, the Virgin proffers a golden ring to St. Catherine of Alexandria, alluding to the saint's mystic marriage to Christ. Cima asserted his authorship of the painting on the small piece of paper *(cartellino)* affixed to the parapet in the foreground, an element considered a signature of his work. The panel formerly belonged to Charles Fairfax Murray (1849–1919), the pre-Raphaelite painter and collector from whom Morgan purchased his collection of old master drawings in 1909.

PURCHASED BY PIERPONT MORGAN, 1911

LUCAS CRANACH THE ELDER AND WORKSHOP (GERMAN, 1472–1553)

Portraits of Martin Luther and His Wife, Katharina von Bora, 1525
Oil on panel

Cranach painted this pair of portraits in 1525, the year Martin Luther married Katharina von
Bora, a former Cistercian nun who had escaped from her convent with Luther's help in 1523.
Luther argued against the practice of celibacy within the church, asserting his belief in clerical
marriage with his own union. A friend of Luther's and a witness at his wedding, Cranach thereaf-
ter became the principal portraitist of the couple.

PURCHASED BY PIERPONT MORGAN, 1909

WORKSHOP OF DOMENICO TINTORETTO (ITALIAN, 1560–1635)

Portrait of a Man, ca. 1600

Oil on canvas

The unidentified sitter in this portrait, painted in Venice in the workshop of Domenico Tintoretto, son of the more famous Jacopo, is believed to be a Moorish ambassador to the Venetian court. The somewhat dark-skinned sitter is dressed, however, in European costume, although the white sash around his waist lends a touch of the exotic. The rectangular package on the table next to him, wrapped in white and secured with a wax seal, may indicate his role as a diplomat or an envoy. According to contemporary sources, Domenico's studio was often visited by diplomats commissioning portraits.

FRANK HOLL (BRITISH, 1845–1888)

Portrait of Pierpont Morgan, 1888
Oil on canvas

Already one of the world's most prominent bankers, Pierpont Morgan was fifty-two years old when he sat for this portrait. Holl diverted attention from Morgan's skin condition, called rhino-phyma, which reddened and inflamed his nose. The banker was so fond of the work he gave photographs of it to friends.

GIFT OF J. P. MORGAN II, 1967

FRANK OWEN SALISBURY (BRITISH, 1874–1962)

Portrait of J. P. Morgan, Jr. (1867–1943) in a Cambridge Robe, 1934
Oil on canvas

This portrait depicts J. P. Morgan, Jr., Pierpont Morgan's son and a founder of this institution, wearing the robes of a Doctor of Laws, an honorary degree conferred by Cambridge University in 1919. The degree was a gesture of gratitude to the younger Morgan, who, as head of the firm J.P. Morgan & Co., provided financial support to the Allies during the First World War.

COMMISSIONED BY J. P. MORGAN, JR., 1934

PADUAN FOLLOWER OF DONATELLO (ITALIAN, 1386-87–1466)

Standing Virgin and Child, ca. 1470

Painted and gilded terra-cotta

This rare depiction of the standing Virgin holding the Christ child was most likely executed by one of Donatello's followers in Padua; the figure types closely resemble those of Donatello's mature style. While numerous Italian fifteenth-century reliefs of this format survive, they usually depict the Virgin in a three-quarter pose, seated on a throne. Representations of the Virgin standing are unusual. This relief was executed in terra-cotta and then enhanced with paint and gilding.

PURCHASED BY PIERPONT MORGAN, 1904

ANTONIO ROSSELLINO (ITALIAN, 1427-28–1479)

Virgin and Child with Cherubim, 1450s
Marble

This exceptionally fine relief was executed by Antonio Rossellino, one of the most talented sculptors active in Florence in the 1460s and 1470s. He employed the technique known as *rilievo schiacciato*, literally "flattened relief." The composition suggests that he looked at paintings as well as three-dimensional sculpture in creating a play of light and shadow in the low, carved surface of the relief. Damage along the perimeter of the marble suggests it was removed from a tabernacle before being framed. The relief enjoyed tremendous popularity in later centuries and gave rise to many plaster casts and replicas while it was in an English collection during the nineteenth century, before Morgan acquired it.

ATTRIBUTED TO ANTONIO ROSSELLINO (ITALIAN, 1428–1479)

Bust of the Christ Child, ca. 1460–70

Marble, with nineteenth-century metal halo

This bust of a young boy has been traditionally identified as depicting the Christ child, even though the metal halo is a nineteenth-century addition. The bust may once have been coupled with one of the young St. John the Baptist, as such pairings were popular in Florence during the second half of the fifteenth century. Executed in marble, terra-cotta, or stucco, similar busts were produced in sizable numbers in the workshops of artists such as the Rossellino brothers, Bernardo and his younger brother Antonio, as well as Desiderio da Settignano. These devotional images were used both in private settings, for domestic devotion, and as decorative elements in religious buildings.

PURCHASED BY PIERPONT MORGAN, 1906

ITALIAN SCHOOL

Bust of a Woman, Perhaps Marietta Strozzi, ca. 1475

Marble

Acquired by Morgan as the work of Desiderio da Settignano (ca. 1428–1464), one of the most skillful sculptors of his age, this bust—possibly depicting Marietta Strozzi (1448–after 1490), a member of a powerful Florentine banking family—may instead be by one of his contemporaries. Secular portrait busts emerged around 1450 in Florence, where they became popular among the city's prominent families.

PURCHASED BY PIERPONT MORGAN, 1908

FOLLOWER OF CLAUS SLUTER (NETHERLANDISH, CA. 1360–CA. 1406)

St. John the Baptist with a Lamb, ca. 1450
Limestone with traces of polychromy

This statue reveals the impact of Sluter, a sculptor who was born in Haarlem and arrived at the Burgundy court in Dijon in 1385. The court was a center of artistic production and patronage, known especially for the naturalism of its art. The careful differentiation of textures and attention to surface detail reflect Sluter's influence and suggest that the statue is the work of a Burgundian sculptor active during the fifteenth century.

GIFT OF MRS. FELIX M. WARBURG, IN MEMORY OF HER HUSBAND, 1941

GIOVANNI FRANCESCO RUSTICI (ITALIAN, 1474–1554)

St. John the Baptist, ca. 1495–1500
Marble

A contemporary of Michelangelo and collaborator of Leonardo, the Florentine-born aristocrat Rustici was an accomplished sculptor. This statue was inspired by contemporary depictions of the saint—young, beardless, and wearing his customary hair shirt—executed by the sculptors Donatello and Benedetto da Maiano.

PURCHASED BY PIERPONT MORGAN, 1909

ROBERTUS DE BAILLY (FRENCH, ACTIVE 1530)

Verrazzano Globe, 1530

Gilded copper

One of the earliest dated globes, this gilded sphere depicts the world as known from the explorations of Giovanni da Verrazzano (1485–1528), who journeyed to the New World in 1524. He sailed along the coast from South Carolina to Newfoundland, becoming the first European since the Norse colonizers of ca. 1000 to visit New York and Narragansett Bay. The globe, executed by sculptor Robertus de Bailly in 1530, was based on a 1529 map by Verrazzano's brother, Gerolamo. Like the map, it identifies the newly charted North American continent as *Verrazana*.

PURCHASED BY PIERPONT MORGAN, 1912

ITALIAN SCHOOL

Pair of Firedog Bases, ca. 1530s
Bronze

These sphinxlike female figures, which originally would have been connected by a central section, appear to be the work of an Italian sculptor active in Venice or Padua during the 1530s. Such bronzes served as functional objects, meant to hold fireplace utensils; their exact origins often remain unknown.

PURCHASED BY PIERPONT MORGAN, 1904

ANNIBALE FONTANA (ITALIAN, CA. 1540–1587)

Bust of Alfonso II D'Avalos, ca. 1569–71

Bronze

Alfonso II D'Avalos (1502–1546), the marquis of Pescara and Vasto, wielded considerable power as the governor of Milan and commander of imperial forces in Italy under the Holy Roman Emperor Charles V. This portrait bust has been recently recognized as the work of Annibale Fontana, a medalist and engraver who at the end of the sixteenth century was one of the most important Milanese sculptors. The bust, executed after the subject's death, was based on a funerary mask molded by Leone Leoni (1509–1590) in 1546.

PURCHASED BY PIERPONT MORGAN, 1907

AFTER MICHELOZZO DI BARTOLOMEO (ITALIAN, 1396–1472)

St. John the Baptist, late sixteenth century

Bronze

St. John, clad in a hair shirt and cloak, holds in his right hand a shell, symbolic of the baptism of Christ. The bronze statue was modeled after the work of the Florentine sculptor and architect Michelozzo di Bartolomeo, who, along with Donatello, was one of the earliest artists of the Renaissance to cast freestanding statues in bronze.

BEQUEST OF ALICE TULLY, 1996

ITALIAN SCHOOL

Panther, ca. 1525–80

Bronze

This sinewy bronze animal is probably based on a sixteenth-century model of a panther by the Dutch sculptor Willem van Tetrode (ca. 1525–before 1588). The patina suggests it was cast in the late sixteenth or seventeenth century. The conceptual model for this panther, with its exaggerated musculature, was the *Etruscan Chimera*, a bronze dating to ca. 400 B.C., which during the sixteenth century was in the collection of the Medici family in Florence.

PURCHASED BY PIERPONT MORGAN, 1911

AFTER HENDRICK DE KEYSER (DUTCH, 1565–1621)

Bust of a Crying Child, late seventeenth century

Bronze

When Pierpont Morgan purchased this bust, it was believed to be the work of Michelangelo; however, current research suggests that it may be of northern, and not Italian, origin. Crying children were popular elements of seventeenth-century Dutch tomb sculpture. This bronze is reminiscent of such heads, in both marble and bronze, by the sculptor Hendrick de Keyser. The cast may have been made after one of the artist's sculptures during the late seventeenth or eighteenth century.

PURCHASED BY PIERPONT MORGAN, 1909

ITALIAN SCHOOL

Pair of Altar Candlesticks, sixteenth century

Bronze

Sphinxes structure the base of each candlestick, one of which bears the winged man symbolic of St. Matthew, while the other bears the ox representing St. Luke. These bronzes are part of a larger ensemble, which includes two further pairs of candlesticks, one in the Victoria and Albert Museum, London, and the other in the Metropolitan Museum of Art, New York. Collectively these would have formed an impressive and extensive set of Renaissance altar furniture.

FRENCH SCHOOL

Pair of Saltcellars, ca. 1540–60

Lead-glazed earthenware, inlaid with slip

These elaborate saltcellars, one decorated with salamanders, the emblem of the French king Fran-
çois I (r. 1515–47), and the other with three interlaced crescents, the insignia of Henri II (r. 1537–59),
are rare examples of the extremely fine, complex ceramics produced during the mid-sixteenth
century in France, perhaps at Saint-Porchaire, a town in the southwest, or in Paris. Fewer than
seventy known examples of Saint-Porchaire ware survive.

PURCHASED BY PIERPONT MORGAN, 1906

GIORGIO ANDREOLI, CALLED GIORGIO DA GUBBIO (ITALIAN, CA. 1465-70–1555)

Plate with Tree and Arms, 1519

Majolica, with green, blue, pink, orange, and ochre glazes

A central green tree divides the roughly symmetrical composition of military trophies on this plate, produced in the workshop of Giorgio da Gubbio, one of the masters of Italian Renaissance majolica ware. Trophies, military arms, armor, musical instruments, and other objects captured after a battle were popular decorative motifs chosen by sixteenth-century majolica painters.

PURCHASED BY PIERPONT MORGAN, 1910

**WORKSHOP OF GIORGIO ANDREOLI, CALLED GIORGIO DA GUBBIO
(ITALIAN, CA. 1465-70–1555)**

Dish with Putti Dancing and a Winged Putto Playing a Double Flute, 1525
Majolica

The dancing putti on this dish (*tondino*) are based on Marcantonio Raimondi's print *Dance of Cupids*, traditionally considered to be after a drawing by Raphael (now lost) made ca. 1515. The putti wear coral necklaces designed to ward off evil and disease. The dish bears on the reverse the initials *M°* *G°* and the date *1525*. It is the work of an accomplished artist active in the workshop of Maestro Giorgio da Gubbio, who was the chief practitioner of the luster technique in Gubbio at the end of the fifteenth and the beginning of the sixteenth century.

PURCHASED BY PIERPONT MORGAN, 1907

**WORKSHOP OF GIORGIO ANDREOLI, CALLED GIORGIO DA GUBBIO
(ITALIAN, CA. 1465-70–1555)**

Plate with a Woman in Profile, 1529

Majolica

Dated 1529, this plate—depicting a woman identified by the inscribed scroll simply as Giustina—is typical of those produced in Italy during the Renaissance and may have been part of a larger service that commemorated a special occasion, perhaps a wedding.

PURCHASED BY PIERPONT MORGAN, 1907

ITALIAN SCHOOL

Plate with a Woman in Profile, 1519
Majolica, with beige, copper, gold, and blue glazes

Produced in large numbers during the first half of the sixteenth century, majolica plates and shallow basins with profile busts of women were probably presented as betrothal or wedding gifts. This plate, dated 1519 on the back, is related to basins produced in Deruta, one of the major Italian centers of majolica production during the Renaissance.

PURCHASED BY PIERPONT MORGAN, 1906 57

ANTOINE SYJALON (FRENCH, CA. 1524–1590)

Pilgrim Flask, ca. 1581–90

Tin-glazed earthenware, with modern metal cap

This flask is one of the few known examples of faience ware (tin-glazed pottery) from the southern French city of Nîmes. A Huguenot (French Protestant) deacon, Syjalon often satirized the Catholic Church in his pottery. Here, two fantastic creatures, one with the head of an ass, the other with that of a hare, carry the palms of Catholic martyrs while defecating and vomiting.

PURCHASED BY PIERPONT MORGAN, 1906

ITALIAN SCHOOL

Stemmed Cup with Two Handles, sixteenth century

Majolica

This stemmed cup bears the scale ornamentation characteristic of pottery from Deruta, a center of Renaissance majolica in Umbria. The light-colored earthenware is covered with opaque lead glaze, here set off by brilliant copper-luster borders. Greek deities of fertility—Artemis, Demeter, and Triptolemus—and their serpent attendants are depicted on the interior at the base of the cup.

PURCHASED BY PIERPONT MORGAN, 1906

ITALIAN SCHOOL

Pair of Candelabra in the Form of Kneeling Angels, eighteenth or nineteenth century (left),
sixteenth or seventeenth century (right)
Polychromed wood

The style of these carved and painted wood figures, with detachable wings inserted into their backs, shows the influence of the early Renaissance Florentine sculptors Benedetto da Maiano (1442–1497) and Andrea della Robbia (1435–1525). Such angels originally would have decorated an altar or the mantel of a tomb. While these two were acquired by Morgan as a pair, they are not by the same carver and likely were executed at different times, perhaps in homage to early Renaissance examples.

PURCHASED BY PIERPONT MORGAN, 1906

ANTOINE-LOUIS BARYE (FRENCH, 1796–1875)

Candelabrum with Figures of Juno, Minerva, and Venus, Chimeras, and the Three Graces,
model ca. 1840, cast post-1875
Bronze

Barye originally designed this candelabrum in 1840 as part of a chimney mantel decoration commissioned by the duke of Montpensier, the youngest son of the French king Louis-Philippe
(r. 1830–48). The graceful composition and alluring figures rendered it a success; multiple casts
were subsequently made for the art market.

PURCHASED BY PIERPONT MORGAN, 1908

PHOTOGRAPHY CREDITS

Every effort has been made to trace copyright owners and photographers. The Morgan apologizes for any unintentional omissions and would be pleased in such cases to add an acknowledgment in future editions.

Fig. 1, Steven H. Crossot; Fig. 8, Arnold Genthe; Fig. 3, Pach Brothers; pp. 24–25, Evan Read; back cover, Figs. 5–6, p. 8, Tebbs & Knell.

All other photography by Graham S. Haber.